hear him. *"At four in the afternoon I submitted to be more vile, and proclaimed in the highways the glad tidings of salvation."* (John Wesley's Journal)

The religious societies soon became so crowded that within six weeks of his arrival in Bristol he realised a 'New Room' for them to meet in was necessary:

"We took possession of a piece of ground, near St James's churchyard, in the Horsefair, where it was designed to build a room, large enough to contain both the societies of Nicholas and Baldwin Streets... And on Saturday 12th May the first stone was laid, with the voice of praise and thanksgiving." (John Wesley's Journal).

On 3rd June Wesley writes: *"In the evening we met in the shell of our new society-room. The scripture which came in course to be explained was, 'Marvel not if the world hate you.' We sung 'Arm of the Lord awake, awake!' and God, even our own God, gave us his blessing!"*

Initially a much smaller room, with sleeping quarters upstairs for Wesley, it was enlarged in 1748 to cope with the growing Methodist movement. Upstairs could now accommodate a number of preachers who helped Wesley in his work.

In spite of being a Church of England clergyman, Wesley was required by law to register the newly-enlarged building as a 'dissenting chapel', thus making it the oldest chapel in Methodism.

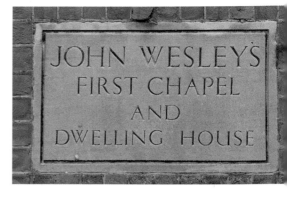

ABOVE: *The stone between the arches of the New Room's Broadmead entrance. Built in 1739 and enlarged in 1748, this is the oldest building in Methodism.*

OPPOSITE: *The main entrance. The New Room, this haven of peace in a busy city, is open to visitors all year round. Entrance is free.*

BELOW: *The stable for the preachers' horses. "Are all the preachers merciful to their beasts? Perhaps not. Every one ought: 1. Never ride hard; 2. To see with his own eyes his horse rubbed, fed and bedded."* (Minutes of Conference 1765)

PAGES 4 & 5: *"I preached in the new-built Room which is indeed an awful place."* *wrote John Wesley when the New Room was enlarged in 1748.*

It was in this room that Methodism began to take shape. Fired by Wesley's leadership, the religious society in Bristol grew rapidly. Members were grouped in classes of about twelve and even smaller 'bands'. They met to study the Bible, confess their sins and encourage one another in living Christian lives.

In Wesley's day this versatile open space was used, not just for meetings, but as a dispensary of medicines, a lending library and a school – all of which were free to the poor. For a time the building was known as 'the schoolroom in the Horsefair'.

The annual Methodist Conference met in the room 18 times during Wesley's life. An eye-witness attending the conference held here in 1790 writes: *"About 130 preachers were present; and assuredly it was a friendly meeting of the brethren. Mr Wesley amidst his sons, looked fresh and lively, and likely to run out his course for many years to come... A long table being placed across the chapel, which had no pews, Mr Wesley sat in a chair on the head of the table, and about twenty venerable men on the benches, ten on each side... aged men that had born the heat and the burden of the day. The rest of the preachers were distributed on the benches..."*

The seats in those days were simple, backless benches which could be moved around depending on the activity.

Preaching services took place here at 5am. Wesley favoured early rising for various reasons. One of them was that an early service enabled working people to attend. Whatever meeting took place in the building, men and women would sit separately.

Wesley preached here

ABOVE: *The box pews, installed in 1930, are an echo from the Victorian era when Welsh Calvinists owned and used the chapel. Wesley used benches in his meeting houses.*

RIGHT: *The 19th century-style pews have doors to each box. The design cut down draughts and gave worshippers more privacy.*

IN THIS HOUSE
ON 2ND SEPT. 1784
JOHN WESLEY
ASSISTED BY JAMES CREIGHTON,
BOTH PRESBYTERS OF THE CHURCH
OF ENGLAND, SET APART BY PRAYER
AND THE IMPOSITION OF HANDS,
THOMAS COKE, D.C.L.,
ALSO A PRESBYTER OF THE
CHURCH OF ENGLAND, AS
'SUPERINTENDENT' AND
RICHARD WHATCOAT AND
THOMAS VASEY AS 'ELDERS' FOR
THE WORK OF GOD IN AMERICA.
SUBSEQUENTLY IN THE U.S.A.,
FRANCIS ASBURY WAS CHOSEN
AND SET APART BY THE
BALTIMORE CHRISTMAS CONFERENCE
1784 AS DR. COKE'S COLLEAGUE.
COKE AND ASBURY THEN BECAME
THE FIRST BISHOPS OF THE
METHODIST EPISCOPAL CHURCH.

LEFT: *Wesley sent Thomas Coke (appointed as superintendent) and others to join Methodists working in the newly-independent USA. The 'ordinations' took place at 6 Dighton Street, Bristol in 1784. This plaque came here when the house was destroyed in the Second World War.*

BELOW: *"Be punctual. Do everything exactly at the time." (From Wesley's Rules of an Assistant). Wesley urged Methodists to be good timekeepers. He gave this clock to the New Room to help them.*

regularly. On 6th March 1788 he preached to a packed house against slavery, *"that execrable villainy"*. In his journal he writes of the fighting which broke out during his sermon: *"The terror and confusion were inexpressible. The people rushed upon each other with the utmost violence, the benches were broken in pieces... Satan fought lest his kingdom should be delivered up."*

Here in the chapel Wesley and the society held Watchnight Services which continued sometimes until dawn. Lovefeasts were another distinctive Methodist activity at which cake and water were shared, and people spoke of how God was working in their lives.

Holy Communion was also celebrated here, always led by Anglican clergymen, like John Wesley himself and his brother Charles.

All Methodist worship began and ended with hymn-singing.

The pulpit is central and pre-eminent in the New Room because preaching from it and 'expounding the scriptures to the society' was the original purpose of the building.

The upper pulpit was for the preacher, and the

lower for leading prayers and reading the Bible. Originally there was no organ in the New Room and so a precentor would stand in the lower pulpit and conduct the unaccompanied hymn-singing – a tradition still observed at the annual British Methodist Conference.

It is peculiar to the pulpit in the New Room that there is no direct way into it from the ground floor. This is because John Wesley and his assistants had their accommodation in the rooms above, and so would come down to the pulpit from their quarters upstairs. Also, whether deliberate or not, the design gives the preacher an element of security.

Ignorance, and sometimes malice, led to various suspicions and strange stories abounding about the first Methodists and about John Wesley in particular. He was accused of being a 'papist' and a Jesuit priest. Some said he was in the pay of the Spanish and was mobilising the poor to assist with an invasion. It was then rumoured that he was in prison for high treason, that he was a Jacobite and had been seen in France with Bonnie Prince Charlie.

As a result, Methodist property was often attacked. Homes were ransacked and meeting rooms burnt down. Preachers too were violently assaulted by drunken mobs. The New Room was at the centre of a riot in 1740. There was violence here when Wesley preached against slavery (see page 7). While preaching in the open, Wesley was hit with a brick thrown at him and later with a stone between the eyes. He was almost gored by a tormented bull driven through the congregation, punched in the face and dragged by the hair.

ABOVE: *The banister rail between the upper and the lower pulpits.*

OPPOSITE: *The view from the lower pulpit. Preachers and worship leaders can be seen from anywhere in the room.*

RIGHT: *Wesley was a student at Christ Church, Oxford and then a Fellow of Lincoln College. He wore his academic gown for preaching.*

By 1748, the Methodist society in Bristol had outgrown the small building erected in 1739. It was significantly enlarged, and a balcony included as a way of accommodating more people.

We don't know the exact seating arrangements at the New Room, but we know that in other Methodist buildings, following the Moravian practice which greatly influenced Wesley, men and women were kept apart. This was done either by a barrier down the middle, or, if there was a balcony, men upstairs and women downstairs. It's possible this is what happened at the New Room.

Wesley always referred to those who stayed at the New Room as his 'family'. The corner of the balcony where the organ is now was reserved for their use.

After Wesley's death in 1791, there was a disagreement among Methodists over who should preside at Holy Communion. The controversy led many to leave the New Room and build the Portland Chapel in

ABOVE: *The chamber organ, built by John Snetzler in 1761. Installed in the New Room in 1930, it is used today for worship and recitals.*

Close inspection of some of the panelling in the balcony reveals graffiti, presumably the handiwork of Welsh Calvinists. Welsh names are scratched into the panels with various dates from the 1830s. The box pews in the balcony, with their doors and high, straight backs are replicas of those installed while the Welsh owned the room.

Kingsdown, nearby. Membership was so low at the New Room in the early 1800s that the chapel was sold to the Welsh Calvinistic Methodist Church.

The Welsh owned the building for more than a hundred years until 1929, when it was re-purchased and restored by a Wesleyan Methodist, Edmund Lamplough.

ABOVE: *The communion table at which John Wesley celebrated the Sacrament of the Lord's Supper which he encouraged Methodists to receive every week.*

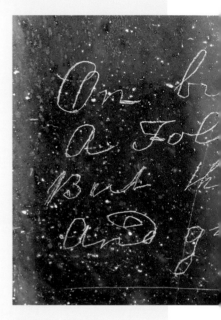

BELOW: *Several of Wesley's 'helpers', staying at the New Room, scratched their names, a prayer or a verse into some of the lantern window's glass panes.*

RIGHT: *The one-handed, 36-hour grandfather clock in the Common Room. It was originally in Epworth Rectory, Wesley's boyhood home. You can hear it chime on the hour.*

ABOVE: *The eight-sided lantern window, set in the roof to maximise light inside the room.*
The lower window looks down into the chapel from the Common Room.

Instead of ground floor windows in the chapel there are windows at balcony level and the lantern window in the roof. There were a number of factors influencing this design. It is possible that security was one concern (see page 9). Having no windows downstairs made the room less vulnerable to attack. There was also a window tax in place when the chapel was built so there was pressure to have only as many windows as was strictly necessary. Also, the best way of letting sunlight into the room is through the roof rather than through the ground floor walls.

For a time Wesley had a preference for the octagonal shape. Some fourteen octagonal Methodist chapels were built across the country in Wesley's lifetime. He liked the design for meeting rooms as

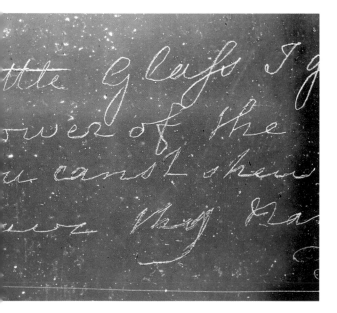

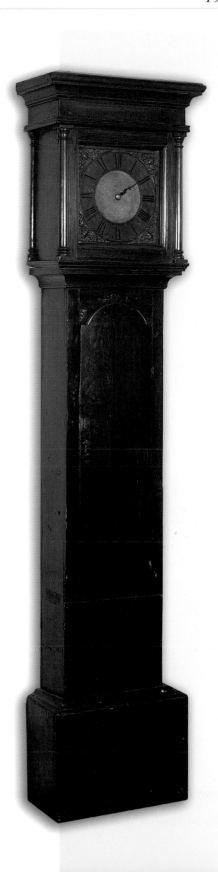

he said they took fewer bricks to build and were therefore cheaper. He also found the preacher could be heard more easily.

The Lantern Window does a good job of letting light into the room. It was all the more vital in Wesley's day when candlelight was the only alternative.

The design enables observation of the chapel from the rooms above. Wesley was able to stand at the window in the Common Room and watch his preachers in the pulpit below. He could see if they were spitting or thumping the Bible, leaning on it or screaming. He could assess the content of their sermon and time it – to make sure the preacher didn't go on too long. He thought the prayers in the service should last no more than ten minutes, and the whole act of worship should be no longer than an hour in total.

U pstairs at the New Room are the
quarters for Wesley, his 'helpers' and
'assistants'. There are five rooms,
around the edge of the central
Common Room, which were used for both study and
sleeping. The names on the doors are those of some
of the leading Methodist preachers associated with
the New Room in Wesley's day.

In these small, upper rooms Wesley's preachers
would prepare for their gruelling, six-week,
horseback journey around the Bristol Circuit, which
in those days extended as far as Lands End.

LEFT: *John Wesley's study upstairs at the New Room, furnished with the chair in which he worked (bottom left) and the corner-chair (below) from which he preached his last open air sermon in 1790.*

John Wesley's ministry was one of almost constant travel all over the country. But every year he came to Bristol spending a month or two writing, preaching and 'examining the society'.

The study room and the bedroom attached were reserved for his use during these frequent visits.

He sat at this window seat, was warmed by the fire in the corner (no doubt fuelled with coal provided by Methodist colliers in nearby Kingswood) and warmed his clothes in the press above.

He sang, worked and prayed in these rooms and met here with his closest colleagues like John Fletcher, Thomas Coke, Francis Asbury and Adam Clarke.

Wesley's last open air sermon, preached from the corner-chair on display in the room, was at Winchelsea in Sussex, underneath an ash tree. *"I called to most of the inhabitants of the town 'The Kingdom of Heaven is at hand, repent and believe in the Gospel.' It seemed as if all that heard were, for the present, almost persuaded to be Christians."*

RIGHT: *The parish church at Epworth by J S Sharp. John Wesley was born and spent his early years in this Lincolnshire village where his father was rector.*

ABOVE: *A letter hand-written by John Wesley in Manchester on 25th March 1780. One of several on display in his quarters.*

OPPOSITE: *The simple oak-framed, rope-strung bed in which John Wesley slept whenever he stayed at Kingswood School.*

A section of the wall in Wesley's room is hinged and swings open to reveal his sleeping quarters. This wide door could be propped open to warm the interior before bedtime.

The four-poster bed here was originally at Kingswood School on the outskirts of Bristol. It is the one in which Wesley slept whenever he stayed there. It was moved here after the building was restored in 1930.

The canvas base is attached to the frame with rope and would need to be tightened to prevent too much sagging – hence the phrase 'sleep tight'.

Underneath the window is a sloping shelf Wesley had specially fitted. Believing that sitting down for too long wasn't good for you, he would work here standing up. You can see where he has absent-mindedly worn away the ledge on the floor with his foot.

SLEEP

Sleep was something Wesley had strong views on. He thought too much of it was bad for you. A long lie-in was considered particularly harmful: "*By 'soaking' so long between warm sheets, the flesh is, as it were parboiled, and becomes soft and flabby. The nerves in the meantime, are quite unstrung, and all the train of melancholy symptoms, faintness, tremors, lowness of spirits, come on, till life itself is a burden.*"

He went to bed early and usually rose (after about seven hours sleep) at 4am for private prayer. He was ready to lead public worship at 5am.

Among the treasures kept here at the New Room is a lock of John Wesley's hair. John Wesley was unusual for a clergyman of his day in that he wore his own, long hair, rather than sporting a wig (like his brother Charles). When he was at college in Oxford the first Methodists began to visit the poor in the town and help them buy essentials or pay off debts. Given the pressing needs of the poor, Wesley felt he couldn't justify the cost of buying and maintaining a wig, nor the expense of having his hair cut.

He took great pains to keep his hair (variously described by contemporaries as black, dark brown or auburn) neat and tidy, and with a precise centre-parting. Sadly for him, while he was in Georgia in North America he was attacked by an angry woman with a pair of scissors who roughly hacked off many locks from one side of his head. He preached the next day and one of his congregation described his unusual appearance:

"With his hair so long on one side and so short on the other...which he took infinite pains to have in the most exact order."

His hair featured again later in life when he was set upon by an anti-Methodist mob near Wednesbury in Staffordshire. *"A man, catching me by the hair, pulled me back into the middle of the mob... Another came rushing through the press, and raising his arm*

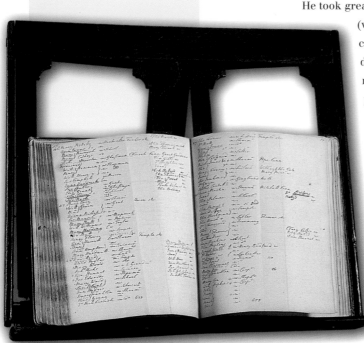

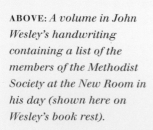

CENTRE: *Part of the ceramics collection held at the New Room. Until Lenin, it is thought there were more busts of Wesley than anyone in history.*

ABOVE: *A volume in John Wesley's handwriting containing a list of the members of the Methodist Society at the New Room in his day (shown here on Wesley's book rest).*

to strike, on a sudden let it drop, and only stroked my head saying 'What soft hair he has!'"
(John Wesley's Journal)

PRIMITIVE PHYSIC

Wesley had a life-long interest in medicine and in making it available to everyone rather than just the rich. He wrote what he called *'Primitive Physic: or, an easy method of curing all diseases'*. A copy printed in Bristol in 1771 complete with its pigskin cover, is sometimes on display. The book contains many simple herbal remedies, some sound medical advice, and some strange ideas...
"To cure baldness, rub the part morning and evening with onions, till it is red; and rub it afterwards with honey."

Copies of *Primitive Physic* are available at the New Room.

BELOW: *A bust of Wesley, of which many thousands were produced for more than a hundred years after his death. In the late 19th century there were about sixty potters in Staffordshire alone producing Wesley busts.*

RIGHT: *Wesley's riding crop survives today, partly because he didn't drive his horses hard, but rode "with a slack rein" so he could read at the same time.*

BELOW: *A three-in-one
letter from Francis Asbury
to Thomas Coke, from
Francis Asbury to Mrs
Coke, from Thomas Coke to
Joseph Benson in 1809. The
address and wax seal are
visible.*

Methodism was an educating force. Wherever
Wesley's preachers went they distributed books and
pamphlets. Wesley compiled '*The Christian Library*',
consisting of works he approved for Methodists to
read. He produced more than 300 books, pamphlets
and hymn collections. Many first editions of these
are kept here at the New Room.

One of the most significant of Wesley's writings is
his '*Explanatory notes upon
the New Testament,*' which
Wesley worked on in his
room here. The first edition
copy (often on display) has a
green dust jacket made from
the material which covered
the lectern in Wesley's
preaching pulpit.

Wesley's collected letters
extend to some eight
volumes. The New Room
cares for some eighteen
original John Wesley
manuscript letters. Also kept

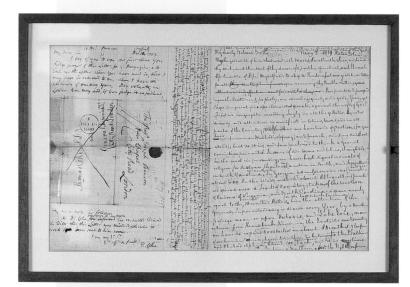

LEFT: *Prayers are
conducted from the
lower pulpit. Is the
preacher above
praying too or asleep?
Alongside is Wesley
preaching.*

RIGHT: *John Wesley's
inscription in the front
of his Book of Common
Prayer. Wesley made
his own adaptation of
the prayer book for
Methodists to use.*

here are letters written by Charles Wesley, George Whitefield, John Fletcher, Adam Clarke, John Newton, Joseph Benson, Alexander Mather, John Pawson, Howell Harris and other close associates.

A number of objects are on display which have been treasured in families for generations, such as the sixpence, given by John Wesley to Sarah Gill for good behaviour when she was a girl of six. Wesley's shoe buckles can also be seen – the ones he gave to the Brindle family as a 'thank you' for looking after him in their home on Anglesey when he was on his way to preach in Ireland.

Throughout the preachers' rooms are portraits and engravings of John Wesley and his family or of significant events in his life. Such as Wesley preaching from his father's gravestone (when he was refused permission to preach inside the church); the mobbing of Wesley at Wednesbury when he thought he might die at the hands of the angry, drunken crowd; the fire at Epworth from which Wesley was rescued as 'a brand from the burning' at the last moment, when his family had already given up hope and were offering up his soul to God.

ABOVE: *Verses in the handwriting of Charles Wesley, the great hymnwriter and co-founder of Methodism. He wrote about 7,000 hymns many of which are still sung today.*

Today this is a haven for exhausted shoppers, and a popular spot for shop workers to take lunch. In Wesley's day there were houses here and a narrow alleyway between them providing access to the New Room.

A violent rabble gathered here on the evening of 1st April 1740 as John Wesley and the society met inside. The crowd filled the Horsefair and the alley leading to the room and would no doubt have broken in had not the Mayor of Bristol, Stephen Clutterbuck, sent officers on horseback to arrest the ringleaders and disperse the mob.

A trap door leads to the boiler room where worshippers on a Sunday evening in November 1940 took shelter from the intensive bombing of Bristol, which destroyed Broadmead almost in its entirety. The New Room suffered a chipped window frame and a broken tile.

Wesley descibed war as "*a most horrid reproach to the name of Christian, yea to all men and women, to all reason and humanity.*"

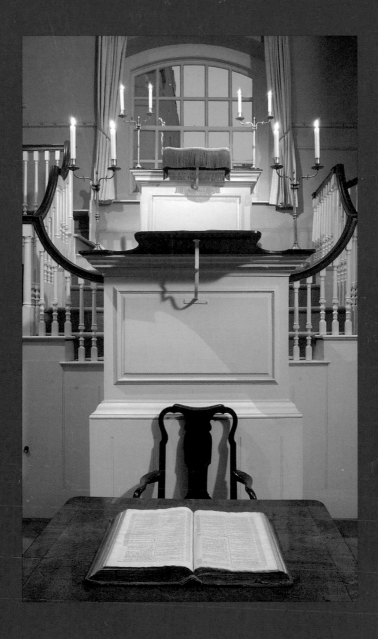

ISBN 0-7117-3444-5

9 780711 734449

D irectly above the chapel is the Common Room, the largest of the rooms in the preachers' quarters. Five doors lead off this room to the small private study-bedrooms of John Wesley, his 'helpers' and 'assistants'.

In this central room Wesley would gather with those he called his 'family' to pray and talk, as well as eat together on the benches around the central table.

From here the lantern window enabled Wesley to observe his preachers in the pulpit, as well as watch those assembled in the main body of the chapel.

Thank you for coming to this most historic Methodist building. During your visit we hope you have heard an echo from the New Room of Wesley's day, and perhaps sensed something of the spirit which motivated him and his friends.

"All my designs, and thought, and care, and labour are directed to this one point, - to advance the kingdom of Christ upon earth."

The New Room
'John Wesley's Chapel'
36 The Horsefair
Bristol
BS1 3JE
Tel: 0117 926 4740
www.methodist.org.uk/
new.room

Photographs by
Neil Jinkerson of
Jarrold Publishing

Text by Mark Topping

© Jarrold Publishing 2004

Designed and produced by
Jarrold Publishing, Norwich
Printed in Great Britain